WALT DISNEY PICTURES
PRESENTS

POÇAHONTAS

CONTENTS

ISBN 0-7935-4507-2

WONDERLAND MUSIC COMPANY, INC. AND WALT DISNEY MUSIC COMPANY

DISTRIBUTED BY

HAL•LEONARD
CORPORATION
7777 W. BLUEMOUND RD. P.O. BOX 13819 MILWAUKEE, WI 53213

The Virginia Company

Music by ALAN MENKEN
Lyrics by STEPHEN SCHWARTZ

The Virginia Company
(Reprise)

Music by ALAN MENKEN
Lyrics by STEPHEN SCHWARTZ

Like a sea shanty

We'll kill our-selves an in-jun. Or may-be two or three. We're stal-wart men and bold of The Vir-gin-ia Com-pa-

ny.   (Hum.)

It's

glo - ry, God and gold, and The Vir - gin - ia Com - pa - ny.

Steady As The Beating Drum
(Main Title)

Music by ALAN MENKEN
Lyrics by STEPHEN SCHWARTZ

Steady As The Beating Drum
(Reprise)

Music by ALAN MENKEN
Lyrics by STEPHEN SCHWARTZ

Powhatan: As the riv-er cuts his path, though the riv-er's proud and strong, he will choose the smooth-est course. That's why riv-ers live so long. They're stead-y as the stead-y beat-ing drum.

Just Around The Riverbend

Music by ALAN MENKEN
Lyrics by STEPHEN SCHWARTZ

Listen With Your Heart

Music by ALAN MENKEN
Lyrics by STEPHEN SCHWARTZ

Mysteriously

Voice of the Wind: Ay   ay   ay _____ ya

ay _____   ay _____   ya.

Grandmother Willow: Que   que

Mine, Mine, Mine

Music by ALAN MENKEN
Lyrics by STEPHEN SCHWARTZ

Ratcliffe: The gold of Cor - tés, the jewels of Pi - zar - ro will seem like mere trin - kets by this time to - mor - row. The

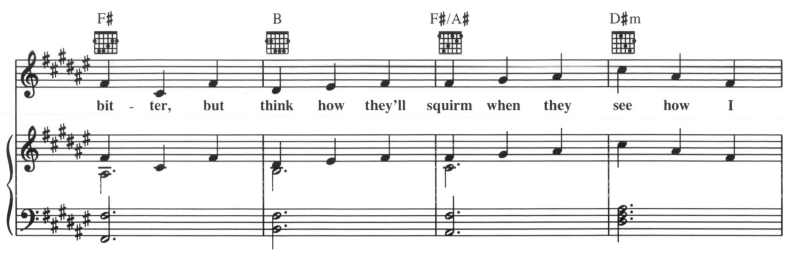

bit - ter, but think how they'll squirm when they see how I

glit - ter! The la - dies at court will be all a -

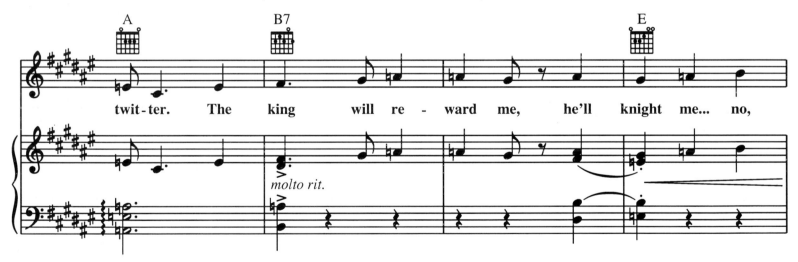

twit - ter. The king will re - ward me, he'll knight me... no,

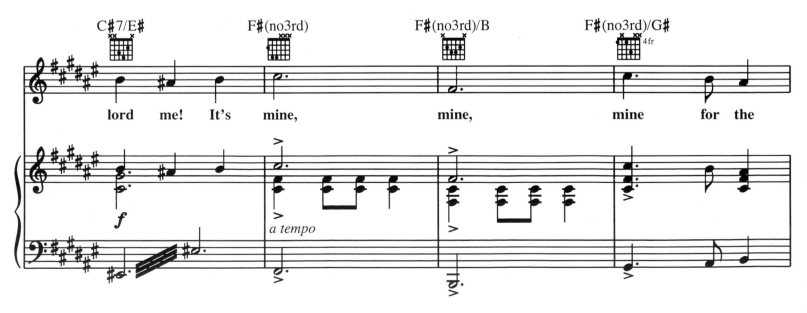

lord me! It's mine, mine, mine for the

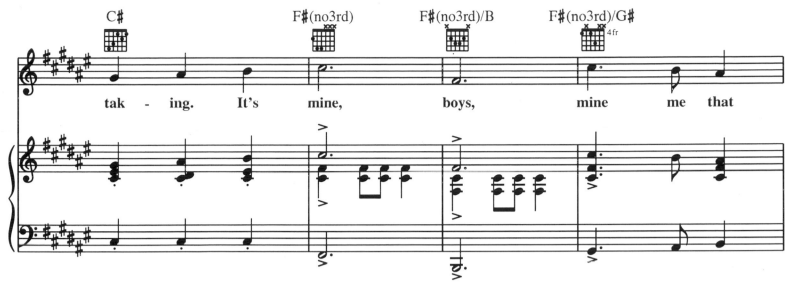

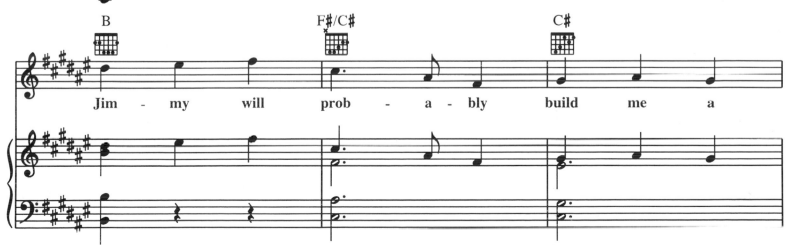

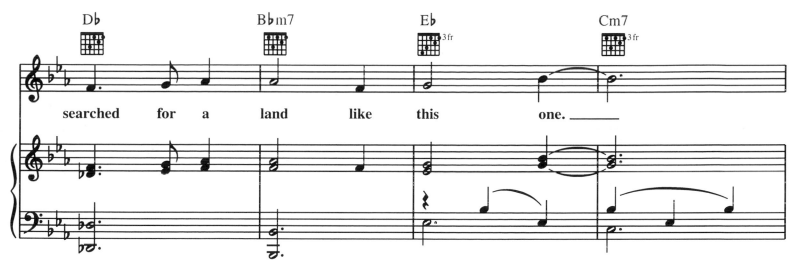

searched for a land like this one. ____

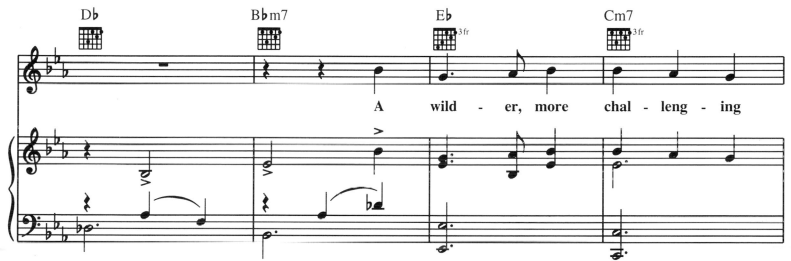

A wild - er, more chal - leng - ing

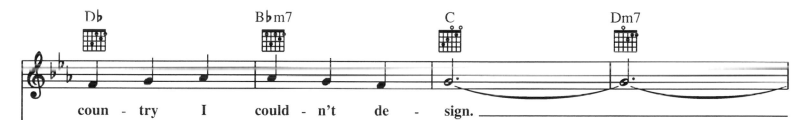

coun - try I could - n't de - sign. _____

Hun - dreds of dan - gers a -

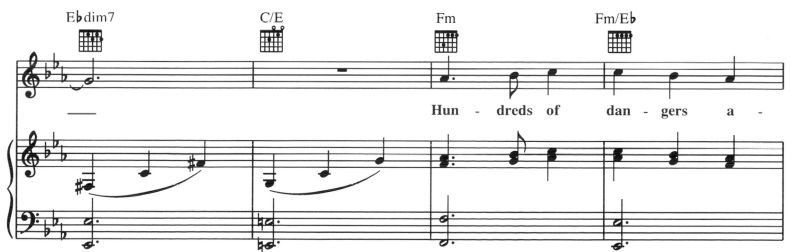

Colors Of The Wind

Music by ALAN MENKEN
Lyrics by STEPHEN SCHWARTZ

Savages
(Part 1)

Music by ALAN MENKEN
Lyrics by STEPHEN SCHWARTZ

Quickly, intensely

Ratcliffe: What can you ex-pect from filth-y lit-tle hea-thens? Here's what you get when rac-es are di-verse. Their skin's a hell-ish red. They're on-ly good when dead. They're ver-min, as I said, and worse. *English Settlers:* They're

Savages
(Part 2)

Music by ALAN MENKEN
Lyrics by STEPHEN SCHWARTZ

Pocahontas:
I don't know what I can do, still I know I've got to try.

dust.

Gm(add9)

Ea - gle, help my feet to fly. _____

English Settlers:
Now we make 'em pay.

E♭

Moun - tain help my heart be great.

Native Americans:
Now with - out a warn - ing...

If I Never Knew You
(Love Theme From POCAHONTAS)

Music by ALAN MENKEN
Lyrics by STEPHEN SCHWARTZ

Moderately slow

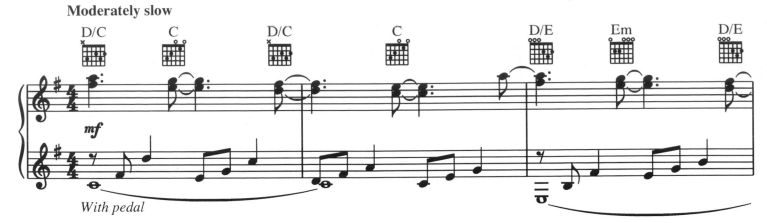

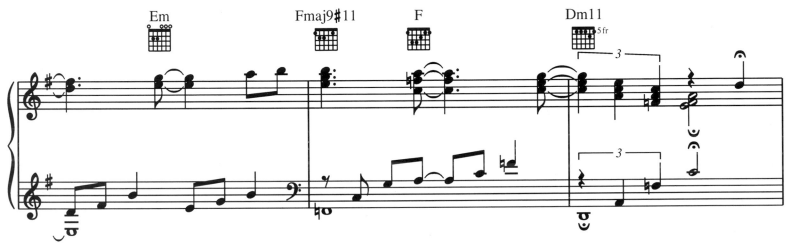

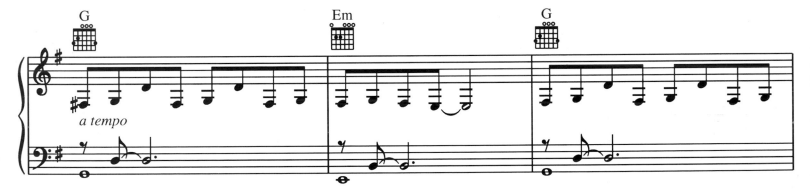

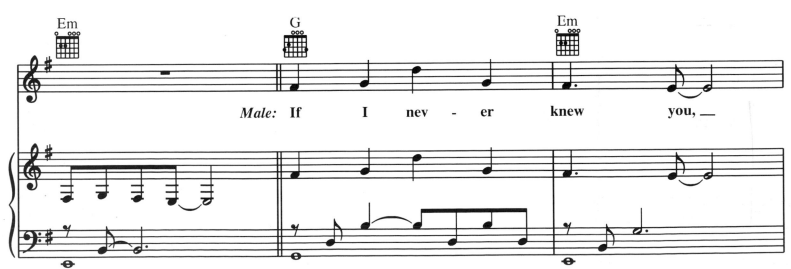

Male: If I nev-er knew you, ___

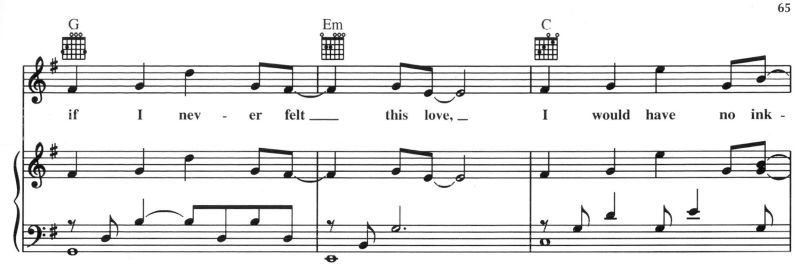

if I nev - er felt ___ this love, ___ I would have no ink -

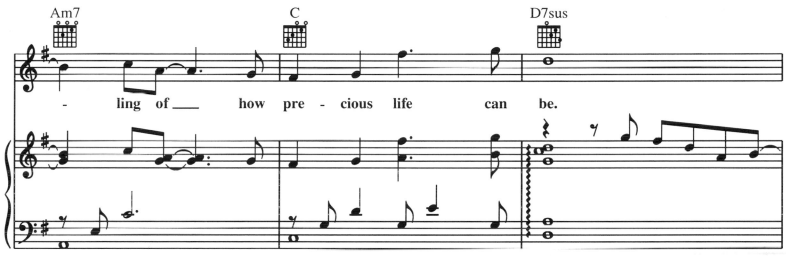

- ling of ___ how pre - cious life can be.

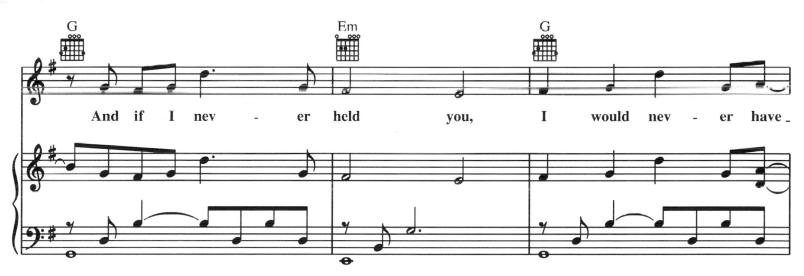

And if I nev - er held you, I would nev - er have ___

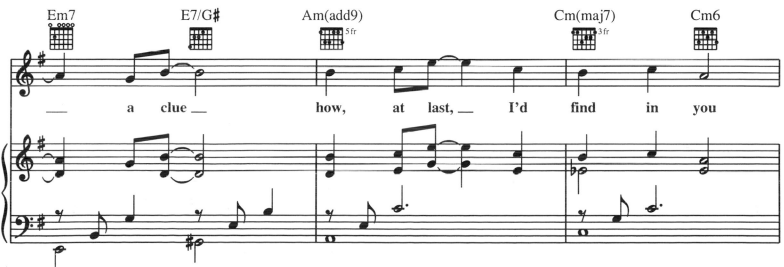

___ a clue ___ how, at last, ___ I'd find in you

I'd have lived __ my whole __ life through, __ lost for-ev- er

if I nev-er knew __ you. _____

Female: If I nev-er knew you,

I'd be safe __ but half __ as real, nev-er know-ing I __